arc of light

---

dark matter

arc of light

dark matter

charles alexander

SEGUE BOOKS / NEW YORK / 1992

The writing of this book was greatly assisted by a fellowship as a Downtown Tucson Artist-in-Residence, an award given by the Tucson Partnership, Inc.

Many thanks to the readers of this manuscript, whose comments helped determine its evolution and final shape, especially Cynthia Miller, Karen Mac Cormack, Charles Bernstein, Lyn Hejinian, and Sheila E. Murphy.

This book has been designed at Chax Press in Tucson, Arizona.

Segue Books are published by
The Segue Foundation
303 E. Eighth Street
New York, NY 10009

ISBN 0-937804-46-0

Library of Congress Catalog Card No. 92-080328

There again there is something to know.

Gertrude Stein, *Lectures in America*

A single thing or word undoubtedly has this two-fold nature: it is necessary to extract one from the other — to transform the compositions of order into components of passage.

Gilles Deleuze & Felix Guattari, *A Thousand Plateaus*

In an hysterical reasoning, the leaf in the air, bird feeder red net seeded, surrounding the tear, a freshened return, solidifying the name, strange edifices burning, to where to where, he leaned and promised, she called attention, to herself in red, a phrasal rhythm denying the sentence, perhaps straight toward, unambiguous *lettrisme*, physics assuming, arhythmic phrasing, still a line still a line, freezing in motion wintered where one river runs a lake birds bite bathe breathe toxic matters unaligned, birth copyright as asphyxiated leakage, a steel line, sounding without, axes turning, enchiridion agape, a far wander to nothing except stirring, aching to be with her, jarring repetitions followed by moans of increasing sadness for unspecified reasons and remotely sensed wilderness, morning preparations the night preceding, a new cup become familiar, a right wing bent causing a turn, amassing fortunes of video bank wiping clean until firmament stepped to a new march, flirting with wisdom, possibly leaning to thigh floating in the air not dreamed or felt smoothly, not for five months until, amassing moneys within the general framework, clogged arteries or more serious vessels before the development of bypass technology, strained carrots, persimmons perhaps over a fence when a child he went walking in a Japanese neighborhood thinking of firecrackers and spinning tops, marvelous road, strident politically events seen through magnified vision of women raising themselves and their children with limited access, through a hoop through a hoop, beneath what one is thinking, for a running start, or wind the frayed alignment, to pursue a knot in the wood, a constructed moment

2 the air twist in the wine glass stem, the figure in the carpet, the blood let in Kuwait and Iraq, step lively, made from air and water, eight million stories, theory was not enough, end-of-stock and end-of-season, the readiness of spring, all is not as was anticipated, the findings have not, in a moment's notice, permit required, a deadened sense of possibility, grapes, in the middle of a nutshell, at the end of his rope untied, until the foliage is yellow and brown, an answer pending in a field of, verbal sessions untended, as foretold in the beginning, before it all became smoothly erotic without men lined up to make matters voluminously multiple and textures ragged to winding, a frightened yet undismayed countenance surrendering its vision of the future to a young woman, of the certain Fragonnards, he stood at attention, a century's pretext for shooting, when food items celebrate heroic bombs in a nearby country or nothing is terribly distant electronically, free of caffeine and underestimated carpet bombing, tainted with perspiration's destiny, a lemon held in the hand, made from what was untenable toward beckoning, amaze us who wish to be denied, merrier than milk, the unwashed waiting in ambush's extremity, and central to her argument for its abolition, wind in currents above us, stand alone, ashen crest or fallen upon hard times the strain makes a spot in the landscape, not at all virulent, present the house as absence, abrasive sediment, contained within only a verb not repeated, asterisk without referent without apologizing, a crater rounded until a sphere, uncertain light the cast of her eye, a cry from the next room quiet like nothing else upon the shelf

3 a long gay afternoon, upon the instant, maneuvering for position, perchance to dream, the spinning as a sign of trust, from dawn to the final moments, altogether too ominous, *A* though it were written, a kind of letter, formed of quick strokes unmeditated, allowing for discrepancies of description, who love to be assembled, around the block with a baby in a stroller, dog on a leash, and the sanctions were working, the redundancy of war, what has been dealt with as an inevitability, therefore already always present with pitfalls leading to the basement music plucked or plinked, the stocking of the larder, an imposition on disorder, the ongoing war, tricked into dissent not voting with the wave, as though it has never been absent, a block of time, a settling into privacy, as a language marks time without occupation, a censorship because we can not face the facts, aberrations are openings, at the drop of a bomb, to beg the dead for assistance, constant interloping, kissing a window because it appeared with nipple delusion, lapel upon a dinner jacket, array of photographs on the refrigerator door catching the light as it opens and closes with a corresponding aroma of changing contents, a start, it simply magnifies the permission, a map of it all, afraid to stand for long in the open, not the solid line of text but the constant variation in margin seen a centimeter at a time caused by the sinuous or sudden movements of the letters' forms, not a meaning without a visual representation, eyes like small stones, the other way into the room, not closed, full fathom five, a straw horse with wooden feet, the sheer inexplicability of an experience, all fiction to me, to one in distress or not

4 an alabaster forgiveness, it's not working, says the cat around the corner, from a moment's orange peel, repeated twice, something something, the name of the napkin, an incessant cease fire stopping nothing, either for the train to stop in the middle regions or not, whether to step down voluntarily, a bullet in the head, abducted in 1981, where there will be a lot of people, with mustard was an option, understood precariously, or without choosing, like the pair of fingers on foreskin aptly placed for peeling graciously, lips toward the sun, envying no one her birth, giving or undergoing, as a theoretical location, arc of light, dark matter bending toward or away from more luminous bodies, quite naturally to women, this somewhere out of context, everything out, upon the shelf where eye's parameter joins light's possible, obliging her with his loving mouth, not a negotiable distance, note predicting rain in a state where one mother lives with another fenced in by discussion, if it matters, a pout perhaps in order, trapping the alterior, terrible rain of bombs every day with no change in the jet stream, fruit studied for its propensity to spread seeds in various strata, elevated function of liver, other bodily functions a mess of medical triumph linked with totalitarian policies in a meadow wanting only to see her riding behind on a brown horse, a practice aiding transformation, sleeping in the cellar for the winter with no waste, the name of Saussure, will be out in the spring, arriving like an oracle, orgasms pertaining to all her habits, for rowing was a memory of nonsense or excess physical expense not unlibidinal, of spirit in a, a class act understood politically, freeing oneself of pain

5 an aroma of desire, the spelling bee in which it happened, on whose bonnet, an array of decisions awaiting a child, without a meditative scandal, a breath of fresh diesel, the garlic in a braid hanging on the wall like a string of eight conjoined sets of testicles, an omelet for two, not quite ousted from power, whether blood for oil or no hostages before an election, do you want to, in a bathroom in a public place late at night interrupted by dancing, a wind enough to make us want to bring her inside, decorations on windows, opening more than one at once but only looking through the second with glasses, first experience of letters as separate blocks infinitely transferable, or without, timely maneuvers, yours for mine, a first time in the garage storage room at five years old, or chicken wrapped in plastic, which two years away in a perpetuating environment, careful not fearful, how is it possible how, alone together leaves and seeds, so we can enjoy, a sexual anticipation of turning a corner into a snowdrift without blinking an eye, toward an understanding of opposition, its interpenetrability, offer her something else with which, a truth function, what other, in need of repair, far flung, forensics aside, need purveyors outnumbered the, bound for home and gagged, out in the open open, redirecting a debt, pry into, as astonishment wields its influence on the everyday, from a moving vehicle, altered by our attempts to make a difference, accustomed to storage in tubes, vibrating with indecency upon or within, vituperous mode of screen refreshing itself pixels alive with flutter, gorgeous scenery going upstream, hitting stride like a baseball game pertaining to the outts accumulating

6 of a wave's whiteness, or a stunned sort of accuracy, from the window's arc, framed for surprise, a multitasking environment from the get-go, altering nothing, an insertion of filibuster, help from the primary contenders for your vote, containing a hyphen, and no one was caught napping, or protested the standardization of capitalization and spelling over a ten-year period, that a people can survive with no food, or suffer one's skin, an outcome of the stated foreign policy, in the dugout where spring seemed like a recently arrived stepchild of the pantheon of sluggers, a widow's peek into wetness, or a filled mouth, the plight of the Kurds in general not just in the highlands, commissioning an officer, by virtue of light's darkened ground, head down, a selfmade man he made good within the space of an hour betraying no one but his dog who was of an age to be rendered harmless anyway despite a certain warmth which had to be deemed historical, phrasing the lyric beyond the point where it disappears, a music of incessant inflection leading to pause and run, over the course of a decision, unheralded but not unattended, an alarum of trumpets forensically announcing a departure, or the shift from bombs to humanitarian aid without sense of what caused the need, upper or lower case, later to insure the financial gains of the insurance companies, as in a letter from *c* to *r*, fomenting rebellion among the companies which introduced letterscaping as a means of personalizing one's language, what most people believe, then, paying attention not at all to the process of rendering a people landless, the way an approach to vocabulary can rob a phrase of its ability to indent into a skull, to take the whole for the whole

7 speaking of mesostics, most of which are prepositional, stunning a wave, from a crowd of people on the loading dock being noisy, a fractured sense of linearity, interconnectivity on the tongue, then someone came up to me, glasses until there is no need for drinking, framed by inconsistency, upon a shore where wave suns the rock of present tense before trickling away, too fast for me, according to accordions, wind as a function of musicality, toys which duplicate the operations of a desert military tactician, storms to distribute sand, having run off the road in a remote part of Africa, vehicle where none was desired, to be certain there are beaches there, close to where the bombs fell, convincing the coeditor, say it was four hundred and thirty two of this kind and three hundred and twelve of the other, what would that mean in a context of indeterminate poetics, who determines the density of the bombing patterns, floating into the deepest part of the fragmentary nature of things, what one never would have considered next, not that the terror could ever be thought to be so close or planned in a corporate office, formica on top, a cooling brought on by a sequence of popsicles, not to not to, charlatans though they be, utilizing a new instrument to monitor the apathy of voters before administering the drug, where foals rush in, freed from any sense of context, an inevitable failure, previous to ethics, alarming how considerate the managers of war can be when they are relaxing at home, an inviolate sense of fluoridation, if the word on the corner can be believed, a sexual overflow, not the last light on the street between the places where they live separately, not coordinated by a sign, of fish, pieces to make alive together

8 allowing for error, responses to presume notwithstanding, a blue streak, talked about for days, when a missile intercepts a missile, absence of ballast, moon enough for child's eye, containing a measure of respect for yellow flowers which appear in the evening as if nothing, a wild and woolly overcoat, to turn one's thoughts over, a hardnosed lumber town, tactfully done, bewildered by the ups and downs, having taken her own bags with her, thinking a circle implied a lack of waste while wondering what to do about its center, squares and triangles into their proper places, efficient as a clean strike on a clear February morning, a painting of flowers receding into gold interstices, spatially, where it disappears, uncertain mouths, a series of notes in ascending order played alphabetically, in a chiaroscuro way, late at night clouded by a sense of just having awakened, riding caps aloft, fears the beginning, laughs out loud only when distressed by screaming making its way through burning oil and bullets proving themselves in fleshy holes, streets disappearing into rain, reaching hand above for a red shirt not a bit like winter, sympathy for the refrain, not intending the vocabulary to be so musical or floral but not having planned for the ocean either, landscape like grammar, everywhere, particulars settling in the illuminated dust, so you know the way light bends around a finger when held before a lamp or flashlight, assuming the moon in a growing phase, a sunned humming intended as diversion, not in any sense randomly formed, intergalactic meaning in one's own kitchen by lamplight, a dream of flying over oceans, immerse oneself, never asexual

9 crayola as a way of life, two colors intending a shoe, sewing two leaves of paper a planned sequence not consecutive, **X**'s marked on a map where previously cities, refugees by the tens of thousands, extending a hand only to find its bones too fragile to hold firmly, not the skin smoothly remembered, cat falling from window ledge having grown older a leap unconsidered, political solutions which do not preclude literal explosions, certain absences in the color scheme, round or yeasted growing beneath intellectual vacuums, had she only known before removing her slippers, not so obvious as one thought, first last and unblemished, nine copies of her gracious reluctance, a child's pattern including dog and cow, laboring until the point of release, wanting to tell the truth, a narrow corridor leading to her, pleasures not intended thereby more intense, writing a way through one to another, never shaking the same stick, blowing a misconception of what the mouth thinks about in a room hiding it all, hiking miles to a snowy ridge sixteen years ago, Europe as a center of exchange, lakeside a site of beached fish, bags of flies and objects mailed as art to various private collections, Chicago needing a bath, at angles from a pentagon of unequal sides lines leading to the field's far boundaries, glowworm glimmer, towels of blue and green stacked neatly, wet hair enticing, gaps in memory filled with a partial language, to love to be astonished, leading to absolution, forgetful of her love of private acts in public places, tracing a hand upon a wrist, the need for repairs as in a country burned and bleeding, attain a state of divinity, removed from one's origins, saying less than was possible

10 reading the proofs, comparing a statement with a twist on an old theme, of thee I meditate if only for a bereaved moment, a father when one wishes there were none, on a green field with white lines and patches of dirt harder than it should be because these are only schoolboys, as if you didn't like him, then a home run, not an itch one might scratch at a board meeting, entering the mural as though its wall were the illusion, a flying banshee, on an evening during the Christmas season with a friend named Fred moving from station to station trying to keep up with a hormonal imbalance, a speculum of otherness, in which, as new as a sentence standing in the rain, before the weather changed the escapees, refuge from what, a choice between a despotic ruler and friendly bombing raids several times daily, a shelf of books more or less leaning in the same direction, all of love bound in a blue notebook, a man whose fingers frame his eyes, playing chess with a timer, not inhibited by a fear of eroticism, a black cover hiding the text, the same color ink as page, because one never remembers the details in the same order or otherwise, a persona for mending, in reply to yours of March 14, where a meeting can only be arranged with stamps, forgetful of history when he cast me out from among his friends toward a desert of certain letters arranged without the requirements of passion, color coded for ease in beautification, when a brush of ink makes a stain of iniquity, or a cheer goes up for destruction on a scale unimaginable, despite the consequences painted in blue on ceramic tiles installed individually, forming alliances with question marks, not discussion but dialogue, or someone else

II

sleeping with lambs but not touching, organs aplenty, free fall, beginning with a sacrificial animal, arguing for parity of nations following an invasion like that of Grenada or Kuwait, to remember only one phrase, sometimes or that of another, taking its sense through what she says, the letters of your name being the definition of cubism, the first page marked with a brown marker as something distinguishable from blue in a nutshell, as if territory were something to be destroyed when power has to do with resources underneath which may be exportable, journals altered before everything settles, even disabled until moons offer nothing demonstrable in the way of tangible rewards a skin can tingle with, translated, composition of an alphabet by committee, trading information as if it were going out of the world in increments not entirely measurable, high density, a kiss for the French, nocturnal ramblings at half past noon, to feel the heat of the blast and remember it as caused by a country intent on liberation, neither novel nor poem, a combination of genres to which volatility was ascribed but how can that approach a warhead, universal suffrage, a sister in name and tissue only except when the chips are down, arranging the tapes in terms of decibels, taxed beyond her limits but not protesting at the physical pleasure of it all, a type cast by a shore, so small that others must wait for the gate to open, entering by rote, announcing the spring volition among the lilacs, not for show or intense suffering, letting liquid fill a vessel, blue lilacs

12 bubbles instead of ice cream this afternoon with shadows, rather striking for a seven a.m. ensemble, not crippled unless she chooses a grip employed strictly by the upper leg extended at a steep angle, sand and rock reshaped by continued explosions, ultimately of no consequence according to state department spokesmen, a quick opening, where hills inhabit lengthy effort, who are trained in rhetoric, with sequence, a choir of Chinese bells, freedom for what is now deemed an autonomous region urged by a balding man in glasses adorned with orange robes, dressed to kill meaning wearing a military uniform, a painted bride, a powerful tale from another millennium, effortless, or disguised as a pear, free of whiteness, a protested war nonetheless even though that point of view largely remains unheard, as if an egg were adorned with glitters of color and wrapped in streamers of bright paper, announcing a free ride, child's hand reaching for rising balloon, fears the morning, mechanically strummed while waiting for gender, eyes wide and amazed, to be learned while watching someone so small, fire as a tool for keeping winter on the run, *The History of Western Philosophy* being the title of a performance, strained carrots, air escaping from her lips held tight along with closed eyes applying pressure a physical joy, appearing without clothes, loving the nature of alchemical changes, that this beautiful new edition of his words, your only commitment to the coast, sturdy, collecting her things before leaving to spend more time walking in a green world, acknowledging violence, formed slowly near the beginning of the experiment, held in one's palm

13 not to blow up the moon, great taste made affordable, her military sinews translated into male terms, like a desert with its craters and seas that seemed ancient, ample, malformed but not cognizant, who are skilled in the lessons of seduction, smiled madly into the heat, from a center not the other way around, comfortable with guns, not the way teaching began, with black fog, spoken while running on a court audible to a few, chomping at the bitten fruit not another piece of pie that brought all this upon us, child indicating rain, not dyed or injected with perfume, simultaneity as an aspect of ritual but not prefigured as were the bombing runs, boring no one, layers of color not entirely distinct from one another, with every egg keeping less yeast, foreign, offering forgiveness to blue oceans, into an enclosure, where we began as in cut and paste until he repeats himself or discovers another presence, crossed out, attending a funeral in which the deceased had never been identified, change of shoes, from an old book which had sat upon a shelf for more than a decade but never lost as in the way the river turns into the earth, the grandmothers, not upset with all the destruction, a parental attitude nearly always a mistake in diplomacy, over the border where we miss them very much, a recognized postmark, birth toward waiting for substance, not to begin another, issues walking, technical information disguising the blood, arrangements of fork and spoon as indicators of integrity, not the wine, always more print than person, descending as a gift, on a train sleeping through Pennsylvania where the early morning woods contributed silver, struggling to be brown or not at all

14 and plenty of breathing, plethora of blue jays, anticipating water, folded into thirds, thrusting, speaking to the window, frosted, and swift, ginger biscuits, that time when the announcement came that the first plane had been shot down more tragic than with the tables turned, frightened of bright lights in the darkness, the horse's tail, nineteen forty-six, when war becomes what was expected because of one country's posture and another's act of aggression as if it were not really about money and the smell, satisfied, announced but not forthcoming, trying to equate dollars with the possibility of words, ashen-faced, not attended as a parade, a cry from the next room child awakening from early afternoon nap in green, the care with which, clipping cat's claws after an incident with dog, eloping, denying the rain as if desert stays where it began forming crystals fine dust settles, asking not more than is necessary, in a blue shirt changing, that shape erotic even when not visible through the wall to the next room, she said, loaded with books to publish and a lack of money, thirty years how many words might that be tomorrow or then, a light illuminating upwards toward dispersal, black dog wrapped in toward herself sleeping, the smell of an oven cleaning itself not napalm or wasn't that a different war this one much cleaner so they said, portraying a land mass as noun, green house with red roof and blue door she made, unable to speak, not a thing a sentence, masking a truth but only one, framed, two ears as though ready, a still line even when judged, driving in snow, imagined as furnishings in bright colors could there be a lake there as well, a small hole in the fabric

15 marking time as a veil through which a voice makes an entrance softly or not at all, black dog with eyes closed, allowing a dare, book divided into letters, what else concerning the door's hinges, alternative to the toaster, melting as remembered from the museum at Hiroshima seen when ten years old not then thinking about war as something to be experienced in one's own lifetime, not the life of sex but otherwise, sized according to prevailing winds, bolder than the north, not to be interpreted except by chemical fraternity, bowdlerized, the author of well-paced sentences, lying with one ear to the ocean wishing it were approachable by hand, in love with tertiary matters, sacred only to the watched, hot dogs never a thing of the past, a case of uppers articulated, not only with the mouth but that voluptuous as well, a window to the room where it all happened escaping, plus or minus, encountering difficulties when working in reds beyond a certain density, pointed, a killing on the market not intended as a metaphor, initial attempts at conversation halted physically, free of the past, made by hand but whose, rivulets, strained to the point of becoming linear again not like military thinking, as advertised, to have left and returned because a case was to be made for more words, clarity alone as an intention, dropped as a line in the water and retrieved by a fish to be, sparked with lights but not electric to the skin, not removed but restated, her witness taking the shape of kiss unresolved, a tension assuming rigidity as a statement of fact, blundered into meeting the wave head-on, full of heart and wanting, there, howling perhaps if not entirely concerned with the weather

16 cherries instead of leaves avoided, spoiled, black moon, aging with doctors intact, childish or never having gone to bed in tears without a reason, standing to maintain tension, fruit for the way it feels in the mouth, tongues for entanglement, returning home after having been refugees the aftermath of war but is it, red pillow, her head moving in a singular rhythm asymmetrical with moans, to the tune of one's terror, as if the daily were not enough but of course, with tail, cherubic, her way in the bath where small boats steady themselves, back to the desert, and the air warming where the rain became policy, musical and malleable, set up as a structure in which rigidity was not impossible nor surprise, a painting traded for a fireplace, who love to walk in green fields carrying sticks but not a game or anything which might be gambled, guarantee the future of nightfall before wanting, steep, statement of loose intentions at least honored in the utterance, so you have to sell and eat the seeds, rolling with someone remembered, skins, asking, turning the station to a woman with short white hair and black shirt speaking forthrightly, steering wheel to steady hands, feeling one's chest as if waiting for a lover not tonight but will you, this phrasing unreliable except as here, for a visual thrill or still life, who love to eat and perhaps take food seriously at least daily, a piece of looking glass opened sharply to the gap in his neck, to have an island available, at the fear of shooting an enemy where identification was not entirely possible, returning the book after much study, under the table where he said he could, meeting you, cat where dog was, loving bread if nothing else, the ability to sleep

17 able to buy more socks, examined by lips, at an austere angle, what my name is, beginning an orange without an anticipation of biting or sucking, music by any other question marking time a made thing compromising the improvisation, hips palpitating, rich fibre, two voices one with melody the other as if grunting were rhythmic punctuation, not broiled or otherwise heated with spice, killing to lessen the world's music never considered by those opposed to the war, brown hair, holding a microphone with mixed purposes, agnostic, fit for a sleeping cat with white stomach never heard the news, no one in the world, her glasses, red a skin or not shared, fully clothed at least until, the myth of self, just saying what the ear allows as speech without a sense of expression made, reception as in love of water, good for the hair and skin even without rubbing another, soul as site, moves together, almost incomprehensible words grinning, the end of a sentence encountered with no color except perhaps red for that moves, from a wound a window to see why the bombs decided this was a time to fly, foreign films several times a day thanks to cable's unending novelty or slow repetition, asking the moon or forgive me, arm rubbed by cat's nose, chimes delivered, photographic intentions snapshot or otherwise, and in friendship, to discuss our dreams as though plurality were possible, peace, echoing easier access and would you, of eggs, enter my room laughing but cognizant of bodies and their availability, stung, a little too effervescent the mind can, to want to calm you when pronouns are ways of spreading the blame, sustain us formally considered as a plea for stopping, milking cows, abject

18 not liking violence any more than when younger, brewed with flowers and herbs measured by the handful not timed or upset with dancing, sing if full of a sound, go, not to remove the vocal cords by aching count of lowered population the war enforces, still the fast food promotion of heart disease, her child and to what degree his as well this morning, to count to fourteen or higher without breathing, from great lakes whose shores make a home for white fish, the common myth kitty, tonight, denoting change in the point at which energy alters form as if movement matters to the final counting which was in favor of apples, my city even though unplanned and not noticed, aches as if she were not breathing there, shopping for polarity, dancing with midnight abandon to where to which, policy within grapes whether seedless or not concerned, salivating, her mouth which gives comfort and seduction, not on the living room floor perhaps wanting, red with exertion, this the war considering, as much as bus rides resemble floating, dinner invitations engraved with small heads pointing to implements, erotic as a function of parts, mouthing the words, frozen, livid, serpentine, challenged by a wave of the hand holding a strawberry still green how charmed we all were, mountain as verb, stunning the onion with a paring knife prepared by ritual, abandoned or let loose, hard but not impenetrable, the strategy calling for decimation of factories and stations of witness the way it all had to be exploded, reporters superfluous to the job at hand, rocks waiting, the hungry a matter for argument on the floor of the body, repeating elements of chance, not the way she spoke or sounded a matter of conjecture

19 arranging the flowers which arrived yesterday, gargling with soda if awakened by flights of jets destined to be over the desert bombing in a matter of days, or was that earlier this year, even here she said and believed the godly interlude, a little left out in love's terrains unmarked on the geological surveys, or bent, a little too intelligent and not supple, an unfolding pink hat destined for children, never a beginning to anything except from the shore where wooden placards make days of words, almost like the same work with woods, as if embracing, lure a science, the undeniable eroticism of language moving from pen entry to page never again undecided, asphyxiated with light, fire the way for sublimation to encounter cloud singing, all changes of clothes allowed for at least a black gown waiting, gender apparent in the fingertips, Joshua trees late at night remembered for its fruits and aromas, or another it might have been, accented, gaining round the near hill the troops encountering no resistance undestroyable, diacritical marks, tuning the piano after an eruption, claiming the oratory was an original act in debt to no one, sitting wearing pink socks and playing the instrument for more than an hour not slipping away or dropping a line, asking a tree where it goes, another room where her attention commands itself, or colors blue with a tint of brown can this match desire, memory too if concerned with forgetting, shared attitudes staring stupefied at two skies, alchemical as in orange, pieces of cake deterring the red fear of comfort, asked to buy a little more than time, not saying anything distorted or a need for repairs, worldly photographs contending for roses

20 arching her eyebrows while lips pout or paint themselves yellow, a he observing or not quite certain of gesture, issuing names like Phillip or Jessica or archangels tomorrow changing, ascertaining its depth by dropping a line, dishabille, where enough hummingbirds circulate to maintain a cycle of pollination but what about water, one of the words a baby has learned the reflection perhaps bringing a self back to an eye but why the sound enticing a mouth, allowable, archaic, enticing a mouth, a part of a part, for the returning heroes or destroyers what welcome hands, blown around the hairs on skin alive, poetics of indirection absolved, never a dull moment deferred, an alternative reference suggested as bait to the sluggish but indefatigable, salt on flour and water baked to a crisp and gold finish, tumbling, red food a bringer of trouble not to heart but haven, aberration of marriage bed to be soaked with ring and again your language, options discussed, disrobed, questions of characters or carrots, ended yesterday but traces, still a mouthful of crumbs to satisfy what means itself as rare fiction, combing a baby girl's hair no two straight and always tangled red or brown, frightened how she said that, toward an understanding of development here and in the world's newest countries, flag black and yellow, staunchly pursued the enemy while wondering what made her that, a father remembered for throwing a ball to many on a marked green field with dirt patches running and making us run how marvelous, not that mantle, now younger as we watch them unrelieved of what haunts or merely waits, knobby and blue it has sometimes made a clean mess or, waltzing the composition home to reverence

21 decibels aroused, relief masking itself as dream deferred, or musically composed as in that poem from the Harlem Renaissance, what was never in repose, a gang's mark on a pole in an otherwise peaceful neighborhood, naughty but nervous her hips unlaced, finally arriving at fly tieing as subject of conversation, a logarithm of belief, entering the room two of them arms descending to last night's ending, or keyboard as subject of desire's amblings, unassuming, engineering rupture a secure footing unwound because of blue politics as stews settle or singing becomes one, though it be morning and wakefulness is yet, such feelings as are built on air, not ever to be intended as a groom or maid of honor, a dream of the largest blueberry pie ever baked, not instructional, attitude delaying itself because of pilot's fear of ascension, indiscretion attracting moss, attending mass, foothold fought for among linear formula red leather, rejecting closure an idea made up while bicycling where the path runs by the river or boats with people standing confer on their marked itineraries, never assuming that she will be wearing blue even though that may with green be a favorite ploy but not an election, withstanding air, jesting, fathering someone who may turn out to be her own altogether or nothing coming without a response more than equal in kind, green not forested or possibly asking someone for directions, until the conductor ended by stepping off the podium and walking off with no words or gestures possibly misunderstood, positing an eternal concept of atoms misplaced, a landslide meant literally after the landscape turned over, villages where landlords once are now tending plots of land, rarely seen

22 even if his dream were only a revelation of rain on water, despite the time, red as if it were going out of style near conversation, joined together in green and white no brakes presiding, extravagances of character driving her to prefer plain vegetables and rice, asking for a statement of purpose or bicycle, eating as an art unspoken, book as proposition in the sense that any utterance proposes a world perhaps too vainly preposterous, plentiful parrot's voice, unsullied, sex as a military undertaking in the desert where families lose and sell for water if not oil, rations intended as preparation, egg not necessarily white as in Aricana blue and green and brown, for whose able bodied sake the paper message akimbo, heard notes as speech writing uses to find form and fiction, in the next room resting her body which makes one glad to have one, akin to mania, troubled losing time a made thing for sake of commodity's grief, fighting nothing but sleep and that less than touching, archly conservative as if language didn't matter or wine argue for open courtship, adverb taken as a river, running the length of her arm an imagined line white with forceful looking a possible explosion of tell me why the fluttering heart, shimmer or letter in love, shrill violins composed to make heard the emotional strain, wrought from war a homeless life one never wanted today the children stare, judiciously, trained bakers flying through pans and pages and quillets, donning a pink hat toddler opens the door and faces everything, nothing held back that is not orange, mildly annoying but not on the street we stroll tell me her hair smells shampoo this logic disengaging itself from voice or where it goes fitfully

23 bound for morning first light attended, anything but round, manifest density, an altitude or by a stream, three breathings well sounded only the nearest cat silent and nonetheless sleeping, steel industry a line of credit, poetry indefensible as a demand, utter strange glottal stops reluctantly they run to allow nothing but what calls itself voice a printed edict, mossy grove, not this country when dream of landscape issues, consonant a tree maturely tethered, axes but not trusting exception practical slippage, not so much of the war or bodies embracing, strictly streams or water runs itself into the heart of a country, orders for accompaniment, whistles clearly even the lines of violins and percussion, aimless with value, astronomy uttering reflection of distance betrayed in the act of travel or destination known to itself, between sand, able to know finish as something attainable in spoken or lived time, read and drawn, isolated planet, missing the movies, eating together with belief, feeling your mouth from all sides, where a science indicates assets of a look toward gray walls, for fruit, leaving sooner the better, wild heaving of hips and thighs a pleasure coded or not and shared, finding them in flight projected as small lights staying here and there forever, sorting volumes in a museum, fresh interstellar news the only ice melt received anonymously pertaining to one's ideas about dissolution's red herring annoyed to a never ending sharp blue edge, going through changes like a tube, your opening floral a welcome divided by darkness no myth here without possible blood, refreshing illusions scattered to rooms tended by mechanical watch, twisted, elegant entrance, drum notions

24 navigation's whispers, enough to think another war or action will demand us if only to argue against its stupidity and twelve types of warhead or bear bodies, a remark in a book regarding a promising bosom, arguing terms of gender, list or lemon, swollen envelopes, burned by chemicals released when bombs burst refineries, self immolation, grief and guilt, blue and white, six and fourteen, green and red wallpaper, buttocks in the air, tide out, concerned with the color of a blue container, met in the aching center of rebellion not turned sideways or head over before tornado took off its coat, looking west for a place which does not stop, excavations age, pond toward the sun, drip as element of musical composition, line made circle proposing, ritual to tree a limb from the dream of its solitude, solid as timber falling no one hears, arms around in a manner of urging this skin's acceptance of other conjugal pleasure, hearing time as a found thing without blue water, surely jesting, once an old hermit, supposed to have liked fish, returned to red sky and sandstone reaching toward it this romantic landscape a learned language advancing on numbness, redolent, pending, newer strains developed from grafts, insects suspended, until she came from sleep in bed and sat before me reading in poor light while video images sang to the animals, whether temperate climates promote learning as well, his insensitive Picasso nation unto himself, slow secrets boiling in oil, less written than understood to be present, photograph no more a theft of substance than letters, record of sensual foreplay, skipping lines, fruit through a sieve apple or pear, aging errors on a field of play, for it is a sound sounding

25 fingering the strings love's meandering free of notation except where music finds time, astral, horns held erect, erasure an act of flinging self to syllable, pears from a prickly tree, not exactly sliding into further abstraction the language making such movement incomprehensible whereas all letters have sound and substance you write to me when least expected, traveling by air a short distance, neither, oak or okra, wooden floor giving in to footsteps either well made or a sign of its age, ready from neck over white breasts to full thighs mine or yours, sneezing loudly despite or because of the attempt to silence that storm, Tchaikovsky for twenty-five hundred dollars in 1891 the beginning, nothing like tonight, a conflict again with people of a different color on behalf of a neighboring nation according to conventional wisdom, severing a head of hair, tingling fingertips on the inner thigh breathing, cup of ice left in place during a drive around blocks to encourage a small child's sleep, yellow paper not yellowing misunderstood as aggression, never a dull motion, thinking they were Presbyterians, depth of fjords not metaphoric, having a nun's temperament or literary mercy, rolled in an open palm one's own flesh no pleasure announced or spoken while finding a window on a moving train bound for some place not remembered or clearly marked on the map, flounder, food, denotations of place or absent, phrasing proposals of nothing but the words therein, asinine, generous, abstinence as a theory, rocks in circles, immanent, trumpets beginning softly conducted by a man with stiffly curled hair extending notes abound

26 loving to skinny dip in gushing mountain streams, the fourth, up here in the north where time sleeps on a rock, forgetting this note for you musical not filled with scribbles, the ear for some a site of sensation to be avoided or held in abeyance, not fear of intimacy but fear of loss of intimacy, psychoanalysis a construct in a room bearing light received through glass above and on one side but who occupied softly the chair central, jumping out the window carrying one's trousers as a teenager, delegated grammar today, to the toilet seat unaided, shopping for recreation or illumination, ten pages a minute the limit of one's concentration unless blue paper, not sexual the distraction which prolongs the act but makes it nonetheless pleasurable between friends, paralysis on hearing the news of one nation's entry into a war it can not win because it is not fighting for anything but can not lose because of its power to destroy all in presence, alas the glass thrown through the window to what purpose but more glass resolved, property lines fiddling with the composer's intentions riddled and ribbons, sashay or fulcrum, previous to sex the thrill of organ notes ascending, not a sign the cloud still, religious pleasure, not minding the rain on one's face or unbuttoning the shirt and skirts ascending against a tree, not cold despite ice forming, where telescopes can see only effects but no bodies, there dark and here bent, roundly criticizing his attempts to treat all things fairly, where logic leaves no place to go but aesthetics, revealed as a minor masterpiece without clothespins, aging electrons, dishes to be washed, living through windows, forging steel without words to direct the machinery and no one came home wanting

27 lightly dimpled in the air dawn makes, fighting a dream's way out of battle where scarves pulled tight mutilate philosophy's young daughters the sons pull from yesterday and make love with or each other, never a time when you are not driving the elements to pasture, fresh fare, joy stick, a lime if you want one, yellow for washing, x over y squared, in case you decide squatting could increase pleasure at the moment of climax, descended, if he thinks she can get away with it tomorrow trying to raise the color blue two degrees until a warming trend tells a story of blunders and wishes, wire whisk, grabbing a tar pit's dream, lingerie's way of working miracles telling letters how to lean, a Gemini wishing to be a Pisces, a note for a number where language can not possibly reveal, refulgent, traveling through philosophy, marking time carving initials on colors or having a reduction in syllables as Wittgenstein considers what can be said without remorse, marmalade reconsidered, a bandit eating a banana, arguing about the merits of respective generals when perhaps all are guilty of butchery, a bishop's decision to make of theology an asp, straightening his tie, straying toward a response to frayed lapels reading lips as if orgasm could be programmed, cheating on taxes, Robespierre considering poison for a queen, singing for a living tonight if breathing could be water, writing paragraphs to be considered as music or earlier astronomy bending light as any utterance bends its own meaning and that of all the rest descending unto earth, diddy diddy dum, binding right, kissing grass when two pairs of toes share curling in a roadside park without rain asking their names or places of birth

28 dithering away time, egging her off, how one comes out of a family with only a pictorial resemblance, squeezing water from a bottle, flesh opening no wounds but sweet sustenance, chasms told, absolutely erotic, even defense a way of waging war which increases the death toll while assuaging little guilt, governing with grace anachronistic as fleece in snowstorms and the destination built infirm, taking calls to establish a reason for coffee, gymnastic, cherub's blossoms, charity making salad, in the city arriving out of breath but smelling hay, talking to hear how letters sound and dispelled of rumors, chastising a wish though no one opened her mouth, pausing to see if the mail had come, combing pastries, generous, avenues expanding but hoping warehouses are not torn down for freeways arriving at other freeways, living Saturday nights in downtown color until Easter, not listed but sought, gentile wisdom if this can be said, missing cats and dogs telling where escaped lead, organizing a strike losing patience for food at meetings, her clothes arguing for a conversation among sleepers, a protector of computer security not a tank battalion commander, disrobing because a similar word was misspelled, joint tenure, neutral boasting, alive in a German town, renting movies to see insomnia through the eyes of cibachrome eyeing a difference in directors, just like family with no intent to deceive breakfast walking light ropes of cinnamon surplus, credits rolling into midnight, uncertain chastity, furniture a clothing for dark night's music hall vendettas kicking balls in back yards making sense of china in closets built from slim wood to remember shapes of rooms

29 calling them bloomies calling, jams to grace her bread warmed and butter recedes, not a horror, taking turns for the dance or worst spelling since Johnson's legitimation of letter bombing toward Latin, returning from stage fright, not remembering the light in a blue corner, and historical characters approaching erotica, gesticulating with the care one gives an overcoat, whispering because sound is frightening, lettuce without, unwilling to release a grasp on an enemy where the name of a war will overshadow her cause of death, situated critically without stroking the fur, foreign she thought of the film based on the paucity of the music playing during opening credits, color unrecorded, by whom, article of wrath, chilled, arousal, microphone as a way of playing the troops trained to kill on command whether by squeezing or pushing or dropping or firing or if necessary by hand no music wanting scores of ampersands, sperm count rising, setting the valves, ask as received, postapocalyptic impregnation a way of making a movie destined for late night until we awaken, colorized motors no power productive free of reign, awkward until brain matures can we swing the hours, paper clip loosened, aching through dialogue, too small to transcribe, promise of care and understanding playing at three dollars per minute in black tights or loosened to changing parts with someone watching eyes held to lips confessing directions to a night lacking teeth, bulging, charting a path in the fifteenth century no one spoke of discovery, spread to the wind's halting music of brass and plucked strings wanting attention to desire, moans to the false light

30 speaking of oneself, sealed with reproof, donning regard as flies joined the general celebration, allowing fear no one called today could it be striped and which, caroling, doing whatever it takes to continue acting for audience consistency, worrying that all this perseveres when nothing can be stated, perverse fruits to the mattress, blue and brown notebooks, self asunder, control everywhere not letting the current fool anyone's drowning sensibilities when blue rings a door divided by yellow, followed with orders where body parts exceed military specifications much the way words exceed their letters or one's wishes for meaning control loosens its leather grip on possible declarations of scale, loose detonations of painted anger because bullets are enough, yes as reflection of tumbrel, agitation coming in threes, precious, counting, organized by elbows, making hardware fly, trepidation before zipper, eye's resonance when forged music plays hirsute left wing games without achieving resolution, stopping a truck in the dark to find out how sand spells illiteracy without forgiveness, whistle when she makes a sound with lips full, not to hold a gun without proper training in velocity, horses loose in a green field when one is caught running for hours when the land is only coming to a hill then water not known until we this morning a dog at her tail asking, milk's color, roan sitting, her eyelashes laced against thigh never an open door, metal the momentary salutation arm raised and bend to hand across brow eyes hidden unwashed and forgetting grace, with meaning a hill

31 frying onions with no remorse, speaking in code, gossip spending the afternoon with tea or whisky, no patience for Pynchon, written which shrieks or flees to the mouth of suspense with no words forgotten during manufactured green dreams, month of May, land of trees looking up to a hole in the sky, darkly hollowed underground where machines mash cloth into wet fibers, sequels of pulp, boiling, cut in thirds when segments compose notes into conscientious fragments objecting to war, phrasing a compliment to exceed sex, the garden seeds spelling underground with fondness, saying only what one knows, mushrooms and potatoes, sock hanging over pipe in a general atmosphere of tidiness waiting for or possibly afraid of imminent dissolution, agoraphobia's mind for movement, absence milling about, a friend's questioning of book's cover as withheld harbinger of dream which can't have limits or makes milk bubble, sonnets to the wind, father's letters in a box, child sleeping without melody, as in, feigning assent, cheers to the conquering heroes returning from where the same dictator subscribes to plans democratic nations may approve if not meaning overflows its box which shatters harmonic construction instead, sharing a seat spinning with tights, where we drove and walked and fed ducks and squirrels and you removed while water mouthed its acceptance and bones never, talking as a place to end, residency where one lives or three feed themselves from bags, joining clubs, lined into left field, strawberries at market walking into crowds sweet pleasure where jostling has sway into morning left undone

32 ladders up and books below, guidance allowed into open doors you breathe, spiritual hiss, acting chocolate, radio waves a voice like hand goes under where foam breaks gate open into field and walk smaller, lines of age, written only to be consumed, marching with instruments, pause a space in the composition for regaining breath tonguing the reed's moisture, deciding whether fears told can assuage guilt or is confession too small to change color immediately given, if this transcription can be read tomorrow next week mission to see electronic perusal, defenestration making nothing more open than glass, tart to the tongue's persistence, shelling peas at a grandmother's home where watermelons are loved and chickens in the back make grace with eggs in infrequent waters, trial as recreation, for clear sight of her inward slant light gives hair on skin no more than rising to meet echo of heard before or told self so everything predicts lisping, accurate when not counting, whose letters used to be written in a hand so small as to extend the act of reading in time beyond what is required sheerly by length therefore manipulating by composing a visual possibility now red now blue no ink lasting, written to occupy space, comments for the living, jumping through a hummingbird's space and surpassing, fire other than this light drawing toward itself, dirigible not something that one intends, vocabulary improving locomotion, factories making underwear a billboard's announcement fades after years a toll, sandwiches on streetcorners, rattlesnakes exiting here, with self described in not around joining terse strings, tomatoes crushed, watered, being a mother not a yard for caretaking

33 whether or not heterosexual some matter concerning fingertips, aspire to hay's dimensions when gathered, going to town meaning the local county seat urban prettiness to ward off sunset, meeting strangers in rooms, jelling into something predicted, a letter it was all and to a friend in Philadelphia questioning a present understanding, wanting what if not agreement, saying nothing not organized as a musical composition but teaching enters somewhere when red food agrees to make itself rigid or impels a fourth explanation, lined across, jumping to beauty, using makeup sparingly, fog in the seaport sensing the past or that we are all visitors, six frogs give or take, until turtles why forgotten or changed is that as a fact, one missing, sticks, folded to points, exhaling, newsroom decorated with red white and blue patterns soon after a war meant to bring the media back into a fold of righteous patriotism sold as information proceeding, won with what blood, having repetition suggest itself, cottage architecture, giving a damn for careful research when her brothers and sisters simply spread words as air parted or bent by slight pressures, legs to be breathless, breathing water so where comes heat if you say this syllable matters, running away to lack, art reserving table space for clear water, focus respecting division championships when the bleachers need paint, having run out of fuel with long hair, as if no one, Japanese ideographs in brass on white wall facing window out to distant redbud not the season for blossom, partial vision, miniature, prayer serving the main course, never a knife, meant to be illicit, short or accompanied by animals being tagged for environmental purposes, hallowed

34 puppets waving, physical ordeal eases terrible spot, cares and forgotten essays, never open raisins meandering all nervous, okra mixed with greens, jasmine tea, her hair spread across belly resting head while giving, gracious architecture sound finds, for a small fee, waiting to be brought to market and birth restoring welcome, not germane, family hearing everything as exhibit A or B when no jurisdiction matters, frenzy to find such reception you say while finding time to speak legs quaking and treehouse baptized, she and she, trying rain when walking this awkward reaching moistens until everything falls, blueberries stirred into batter at last possible moment, sensitive hands measuring sugar resolving for written, dug out, respecting the military mind if agreeing with anarchy through fear, courageous desire to reach a public speaking anything but plain and eating toast without marmalade as sign of pain refusing succor, red wound, pushing her stroller with doll's change of clothes waiting, seemed hesitant accomplice in sun's full glare toward morning if not a move backward when nothing offers, beat, without any language, making up blues while baking muffins understanding each as leading to desire, where books on shelves change color over decades, acting a history, rolling hills surrounding water stone bridge tells, two exchanging fluids, deciding to swim without anyone having been introduced, moral dilemmas when liberation seems to side with the increase of capital interests where incessant bombing is taken as the answer what questions now, for whom, one story for consumption, muddled inconvenience, graves, more than thousands, eating with suspended malice

35 dividend a blue pond no currency resembles, positive rumblings the grass hears, portals not yelps, old blue hill mistaken for moral introspection gone pale in the face of no face expressing numbers anything else lost and red fire giving body heat she loses shadows and loves the inconsistency, dancing there, on a street where trees live and past walking, no erosion, either or a pencil readable in lead this, arguing revelation to teapot, never setting fire to water without reason for light not violent ends as in oil fields burning to keep bombs innocent, lost haven without toil, genie's light, arched eyebrows haunted by wisdom untended where great books inhibit sacrifices joined to loss of green, pointing out facial parts, old man beyond, whisper thing rocking long boats, aerial body attracting steady look around leg to back scratching until return senses silent, with athletic shoes, dated by rings, ambiguous about where the light had come from not taking prisoners moving shyly to its origin, really dead, fading from radios listening ears abroad turned in to assonance, tuning forks for no scale hummed to madness, just this side of uncalled living, from Memphis strumming Egyptian felines taunted elegiac, prying loose, only glasses remembered of a woman with white skin and red coloring wearing black and pigeonholing people without knowing them in clay or asunder, hair as flower, science generous before proofs of its honest abeyance, orchid, not supposing to gifts of paper, between two rises rest as in placing head down and breathing, minding her scent, gorgeous weather, asking a different question of the sound, straying within her mouth, aloft, winding loving a stiff end, remorse to whisper

36 directing traffic with a wig, his favorite meal dominated by the color green but equally spread among textures, plop plop, a mist conforming to four corners, waiting outside in humidity while dinner thawed and daughters ride small cycles borrowed from another's infants faded pink and lacking momentum, air only, wanting to read something old and maintaining certain distances between words licking silence between curves of literal intensity carrying radio to fruition among grasses variegated in low lying fields, listening bent toward toes, free of growing vines, nowhere the smell of postmodern drawers holding old buildings in suspension, gallery of brilliant color in rectangles furnished and framed, reserving a moment, covering your windows, elegance his watchword with torn paper and the desire to finish nothing before beginning, shortening the path, speaking of art not why, hungry, dead again, curved, loving, as a fan turns air and moves it down to replace stale smells ending up somewhere else standing alone towers too obvious or round corners buttoned in place again, a town where dust settles, personal struggle moving spirit to answer what, unblemished parables, ripening, only two or not yet that age and feeling language on the tongue challenging two possibilities meaning more than color, blown into the corner where tongues left the flavors dancing, suspended in its liquid utterance or just the touch of flesh, orange in a distant thought, juggling to her laughter, music for mambo in shadows leaving English for something brown moving blue, as an onion peels or rings with no heat, three times eight plus six, dining with family, cooling the water's tension when blue shirts float

37 appearing green but no fresh plumes, cooking altered for circus torture mothers pushing eyes to intervene and counsel preparedness for war waging spatula supplied nonstandard relishing silent swallows waving flags, prayer showing wrinkles, lists studied to relegate nothing to a swamp, where we wash ourselves and how long miracles remain unknown, devotion to light, darkly dependent or cast into melancholy sweetnesses, yells for no reason, seventeen years between books and this hand keeps forming letter shapes with no promise of immortality, permission to wear dark glasses, wiser thoughts prevailing by morning, until she married Joseph and the bets were on again pertaining to absolution, not dangerous excursions conceding reluctantly the damage fresh spices make to our hearts, not meeting with eyes, intruding the folds move slowly toward more inward where trust lets clench inhabit climbing tones and decibels tonight, coming to ruin all the plans, justice raising lips to accept wine flushing with solace, hands in the air carrying signs to move against the fighting when politics assumes clear sails or avers, the only order maintained in straight and curved lines not music still calling sound to whisper ear's edge grasping, earned intimacy, consolidation of muscles in the grip of another body's habit of solving puzzles with the skin, yelling and spitting into a microphone, singing to sell juice, calling over lines north and south hardly enough or replacing sight and hand ask me for friends to sew color onto knees and wrists telling what the utter shows grace or broken nose ever willful, going to sleep with white space, a number in memory of street dance

38 wondering if those who write mind one more or if spirit wastes shame one hundred times tracing, enough music tonight, joyful yes, click click, turned until electrically spurred movements are all that remain, healthy color closer changing formed around what here and sundry moves, blue above below, less than, flower in porcelain dolls in a drawer saving for grandchildren and closed to reason, mile away more crosses the road, having met before the tulips, carefully removing one three eight and more until nothing inhabits breathing pulse not calmer until latter, public space, not marching anymore but singing with coat and tie young man moves with no grace but sincerity, feeling a library as another battle and is everything so, looking straight up beginning to sleep so it seems snow would welcome eyes to never burn the past brick by brick, less an apparition, legs thin and supporting piano played note by note unwritten and all equal to her fingers short and quick under the scale, removing leaves, solid black of wood, large and colorful, gaining admittance to theater of war with its laughter and arms blown through the air triggers ready for walking the wounded home when it can be found, chilling, laced but removed, blue pillow on pink, remembers her hair, where a tent stayed for one week entering mountains and believing yellow remains, typically enigmatic, decimal point interchangeable if based on intuitive leap, discovering infinity with red hair, putting one's hand out as if the thick color had form but only light as fine moving earth to round off the bowl where it bends the sky, no gesture unopened, rife with meaning, firing a name into clay pressing metal letters, turning in sleep

39 never no war raging and birth, echoes out of the rising canyon word calling itself fugue, between places where focus replaces sight, jazz quintet adding trumpet and saxophone to the piano trio improvising in full knowledge of Hawkins's *Body and Soul,* Jersey City and Jersey cattle, private property surrounding a lake while another is open to everyone and anglers decide where to turn, pleasing with skin and lips smile in front of tooth's gap, a time for honesty despite the propensity of the language to continue, a saint's admission of guilt without which no stone carries a secret, stores named after miracles, decorative arts, the tendency of computer books to be poorly written and designed, never minding the cold, ax edge, simultaneously uttering insanity and Mormon boys in white shirts and black ties crossing the road, whether or not one cares for the elderly, double dip, predicting five days of sunshine and thick water emerging from pores whether clothes intervene or she greets, road entering those mountains, chance to discover what has already been called, nor enough money to fight the spread of killer bees perhaps amoral telling then, the route the word takes no projection can make music follow or sue for righteousness therein, asking permission of mothers and grandmothers, winning streak, judging those who fight how can those who make decisions allow the obfuscation, small as hopeful and reading allows, resting another day, feathers in a nest above wind blowing water, adjectives, celebrating for those who left early fathers and love's salad, remembering she went to Mexico and travel overtook living with silence, what he sees asking blue feathers, hat and handbag

40 refrains asking to be raised a third or ascend peaks and scales, common markets determining currency outliving the war, lowering self to be seated here where pleasure soars, guitar searing as one past includes a note of pleading urgent surrender, pastel stripes, borders or red ladies answering no demands with a common thread, holds off while showering astronomy's distance through a small window, several criteria beginning how data moves, more direct and faster with random access, swollen membrane cell's decision to enter day, travels over the head, naive or contested, plus a blue leaf settling when air shows us a strong face mouth open breathing to live around the hour jelling atmosphere when earth takes what is given, looking numbers away a person bathes without assistance, filling the water bucket where the dog drinks and bathing in the dark, chlorophyll such a sight shuddering, orgasm leading to shock, definitely a mild manner in the strategy room where plans for the bombing are directed and applauded, diagramming sentences until the bell cracks, jars of sweet marmalade before the first sign of restlessness, when arms are spread to remove a coat and identification wrinkles, personality determining wave, occluded until fog breaks the bay waters allowing the appearance of hillside flowers before noon, dining along the coast on soup, walking through a Zen farm with two notions of grammar, priestly embrace, single disappearance, pane of glass needing replacing or at least a coat of paint, out of order never a question of massive apples in the morning, a break in the studied appearance of her letters, with hair reclining, reverent daisies

41 jars of fruit, giants, illumination faltering but so pretty green and red not even snow ground's elixir cause of injury make me want and dry tomorrow, catching a walk with nothing hanging, a shower every morning but night ever loves peace, from bountiful where state lines cross the water crying with rain, credit denied, up with outs exceeding runs and lines fearing removal tied in knots when everyone looks from above, down, changing clothes in a storm, ready for water before sleep, judging the density of ink, brass lined up in chairs and photographed without playing teenage variations on a lip unprotected knowing only the way trading complicates embouchure, hand forcing it, flying above Texas, elegance considered in the shower, cocksure, long for the sake of being long because it all continues whether in or outside the margins precious straight lines a teacher said must line up visually whereas another here believes the individual shapes of letters determine the web's ability to attract love in the park virtuous ecstasy, machinery magazines business keeps the fly in the bottle, professing war as philosophy's handicap, worn with no effort age makes, loving men and having women for friends, driving a yellow car at least until sight returns, a week or two until Canada words return me, saying an ache is physical when he leans on her why accept all this against a wood wall outside nails creak and hands take flesh together the sun is cool today inside where no one sleeps, shaking a head yes, balloon contained by ceiling, having outlived one's parents in time alone, grey chairs undetected when a moment's crumb disappears physically into the carpet where panting increases later at night, loose

42 clear part of egg white turns dipping its head in decisive conduit notes formed in a crescendo for french horn, the main course fish, not liking the sound of what can not be grown from seed, leasing her air for a ring's toss in the air, planned community, squeezing around a woman with two children in a health food store extracting yogurt from the cold, arguing with ascension, speckled, brought to bear on blue, milk's satin, walked by an exotic tree with large glossy green leaves and enormous flowers somehow disabled in the humid afternoon, stained and removed, stock in tirade, murmurs of weapons moving into the morning across another trench having so far encountered no resistance doubting the warriors' presence in memory, legs thrusting to air in the park swing, cable extended, warmed by a premonition perhaps eighth notes in a line paced perfectly as if the piano counted with a yardstick also, honey dripping down a leg, eleventh hour moonlight sending a passionate message for light comes in threes tonight, shot holes in skin, falling in a crease with a pen and no paper lined for the ages, almanac of considerable time, calling aloud a made-up name for speech is later, yellow chair, at every turn ambiguous, escaping the foam in from riptide a dog named Leonardo bitter only because later a white powder friend disappears from view and somewhere in Iowa plays an old song for his keeping time with himself, not getting any better, thirds understood but misheard asking to be placed in an urn, her body waiting next to a child, in the next room or down the hall which house remembers while words ensue, red bikini sky in the window, an aging mother forgetting to live

43 turned, on the premises matching color with wind, collaging dream with deference to green hills, jamming the blues, chords hung in disrepair without fear of hurling lightning among echoes, forensics teams trading places with ballerinas aerial the direction investment leaves organ tones surrounding wine, actors speaking *full fathom five*, assuming intelligence shows on charts where red and blue lines concur if lethal, one followed by two another interval from the tonic taking a melody into modal increments expanding the length and size of notes until abstract passion falters or bridges a scale, in debt to the entire concept of money, memory's lust, nether arpeggios, living will or will not a suspect of a fish monger, five spots, feeling that your skin is still there continents explore themselves while witness loses breath, ink blot, prepared to meet her full bloom departing where ocean touches lightly costing nothing, while a woman packs bags for a departure meaning the light returns to child sleeping for herself, avoiding work on the bus, better than molasses, skillets packaged with instructions for cooking storms and waiters wanting, fleeing from what seeks winter's blessing, stealing time a lost thing, frowning the light joins tumbling chords, traveling from Spain standing airports with boomerang technology voice resounds, aerial corridor hummingbirds through colored hoops trembling in the botanical gardens raised to me your skirt's sheen back to under, within, warmly confiding the luxury of socks, cream cheese only recently admired with grains a bundle of promise, transcribing furiously, war settling into memory where death's music wanders into absence, finally gazing at the light

44 perturbs the balanced dust, two legs bent, still or perched, garage band, two rooms built to order an opening of family considered as gathering, wilderness at the traffic signal, clarinet or toe clips, purple bell, the cool question of legitimacy, fruit punch, jeans where there are legs to hold them, clairvoyant while radio signals falter or aluminum rings church bells tones less than a mile ample security, males notwithstanding torture in the burning oil fields, mates calling in whiles of two and five note bursts, mine to hold and harbor where the sails fall to water, gratuitous good taste, which the window loses as air, largely within the novel's stolen space where a reader lives to listen, to make whole with clearly seen things, her musicianship, decorated for flying more than enough bombing missions, finding valor in the leaves, ten speeds, raised shoulders, blue steam still riding more than ever within the determined bonds of friendship the strength fails nothing to tell red whispers, the way Southerners love iced tea, singing on another continent old river's peace a man and instruments, reading every other comma not a foolish bone, bawdy green underwear with patterned perforations altruistic tones, jogging in place who do mountains pass soul's citation, in an atavistic manner, exchange of water, offering the moon an apple in the face of right wing confusion, leaving someone alone when names are mentioned, prince of persuasion, ogling the flowers wild at field with a leg in the world, letting someone own a word intact, the waves, the black, moving in spirals toward up, blank walls for murals residing to determine desire's address not hollow, brick transgression a structural bellows of lore

45 Thursday stranded in the market with a cart bent toward avocados ripening, disrupting the flow of water to a body measured high in response and resolution, herbal vision, Mediterranean memories of friends, northern latitude, repairing an automobile on Lake Superior's northern shore in late spring a breakdown with someone else expiring, short count, altering nylons on each leg stretched with tension and no lack of fingers, wrist burning, blowing left to right, armored division, blonde beauty in the arms of soldiers marking a heroic return from technological dissipation and kill totals, asking to be held in the mouth, missing with a fastball, minus one dog replacing a family plan in May when it has rained a day and a kiss exchanges fear for surrender, joy's solid remedy, marketed without respect for gender, walking upstairs in a black dress if you call him anything with silence, teaching formulas, apprehensive, gazing or flying toward stars in a fully equipped ecosystem massaged by a Texas billionaire and a theatrical cult leader a sign for obedient luxury in a current century saying nothing unless books tilt on shelves assembled from spare lumber in a rickety warehouse lending itself to sundry purposes previous to a disappearance in favor of disruptive highways, ten rectangles and a net gathered for a game with balls, estate selling itself as leftover living, sitting in one's own house minding one's own business playing one's own piano complicit with crime, closer than ever, appearing without a warning and glistening skin, bullet holes and explosions meandering through a significant part of a middle continent, proof without pudding

46 on a beach in full gear wondering why a rifle was not transcendent after kindergarten, systemic failure or nervous keyboard, thirst in a tower with bells upon toes, certain sanctuary, in third place at forty-six years of age through a glass tube, oxygen plentiful, a stroke of white paint in a green field with no sense of rupture or violation except that which is political rather than of the body, loving to be astonished or represented in letters historically divided into upper and lower with a middle replete in apology, a child's gestural drawings articulated as persons in a context of memory, five cent parts, withholding accent marks in a central embrace, hips in position accepting wonder or faltering in the middle of one's voice, happy as an act of hostility, knees raised, the serenity or scarcity of combat knowing which businesses will not die, wondering why the pink robe requesting an encore or living apart, paid for speaking to ears, sending work to anonymous boxes, numbers lying together, hair remembering an ear in linens trusting a heart to private pulses elevated to serenade, piano notes allowing the air to speak, peaked rims hiding, gently rubbing a self made meaning into the ink's oils before printing an image, believing her story with all the pauses in its telling, not enough of rock and water, walking home, regaining confidence in words, spelled with a sense of direction without fresh air in a video landscape, early explosions morning or strange beds colliding, playwright facing the camera with some trepidation, shepherds' hymns crying alone without women in a prophesying light remembering Jesus banned the rich from a heaven wars never accomplish

47 budding in the spring not counting whispers of impropriety, with religion's blessing if not water sprinkled with caution and without generosity, pregnancy stripping itself of myth, meaning's improbability leaving only aesthetics in a desert where rain occasions a rising smell of diesel, dieing on a cross or living across latitudes parents remember like the ocean in the west, choosing a time to visit the water with a small child not turning red this year with shoes to match, imagining life as an artist forgetting first solos on wind instruments before an audience impossible to reconstitute, generating heat from friction lips entirely occupied, ribs exposed on a mesa protected reservation a standard cry of horses in winter passed gingerly by 1960's automobiles, wearing rain as an expression, pleasing to an expansive skin flirtation allows a flower, waving the flag into battle while sales figures double, unable to feel a breast's movement breathing all night, cut hair repelling deer, a two-year-old's discovery of ice cream in a shrinking economy wherein parental desires are delayed to appropriate moments, wanting flowers at any time, sitting with such care one dreams tomatoes on black and brings the weather back, dialysis forever giving structure, in some way entirely distant and admiring of what transpires between mother and daughter although living in the same house and sharing closets, distracted by your mouth's fluctuation, metaphorically allowing sonatas as landscape most likely mountainous without storm, eating prayer in a borrowed vehicle, writing outside the lines, robed and singing as though salvation plants a root in the throat free of desire and idly consuming

48 integers holding a tongue in place, trying to confuse the digits while respecting the ability of hand held mathematicians, blue faces preparatory, watching a friend walk on a street disoriented and skipping steadily arhythmical breathing hard a telephone call dying then exactly then, upon the face of a mountain with a teenage friend waiting for a map lost where our voices fell, changing into a father, allowing rough language, wishing you approved of these friends and their shapely letters, a chance for time to catch up with dark matter not until suffering expands close to its limits, loving to look at the sky, losing faith that governmental propensities for war will ever dissipate amid red mornings never alone again and child's eyes aware of more, below mascara wanting to collide, men sitting in swiveling chairs bereft, making pretty an industry of eyes and cheeks and blood, wearing black suits, loss of hair an attraction in middle regions, human more difficult with days, blue and green, shopping for exercise, foreskin disappearing, attaching dust to friends and telephone reaching to satisfy past and present shaking of the will to understand why nothing untwists or paints itself red in the night only holding your waist and expending flesh or exhaling in awe simple and stupid fear of everything, shaded in memory of blue water with no rowing, upon the leafy flesh of trees, with her above the ground but not far climbing, asking forgiveness when one wants simply to turn the other way, seeking simple bowing on the cello with a face promising no more, a mound in the shape of an animal by the water fresh with desire floating or wading in but not noticing the sharpness of language, laughing through lace

49 celebrated by a best friend for a capacity to love and he knows that desire to embrace a color or fall of water when everything seems yellow and capable, smell of an inviting house where an aging woman known remotely and intimately makes a home town possible, gently touching with both hands a shaft of light, hunting for painted eggs in tall grass on a hill, finding a way to express lack in a field of overcompensation for clothes of a similar color where language is used but seldom felt as cellular, not a victory, winged static, designed to respond abundantly, falling forward into technology writing a program or batch of phrases to imagine a universe where bent light is generosity and peace with no desire for stasis and frankly antiutopian dreams recognized for their erotic instability, banging, not loud but far, stripped, joking, music from a refined oracle piercing spirit, rage rare green, replacing friends for changes in location, attaching wires to make a music of brain waves, wanting even illness to make a contribution finding rocks a given, disappeared into a newly forced politics pivotal, growing child and shrinking parents, keeping the knowledge of violence a step away, purple with red dots, chinga chinga root, dialing one two three four, never having to start over with thigh resting on thigh sleep blessing energy resolved into loss, nowhere to turn that does not simply grow old and die, bless with pilot's eyes, turned a camera to a quickly rising and spinning hummingbird green breast glowing, language of language, good things getting twisted, salvaging a word from a possibility raising sound, needing a nap, the actual weight being carried

50 petals resting on water, eating an apple because it feels good in the mouth, counting spaces between lines, trains as bullets moving always arriving, humorous shapes of letters, s a difficult turn to consider sexually, absorption an artifice in one place posing, frightened of insects flying into the swimming pool and drowning without noise, potatoes ripening in order, dry cleaning day, only books about whale and dolphin frolicking a naturalist's repose to green lines, clay torso, boots, light shade flowering up without an equal distribution of light, atmosphere besmirched with burning oil fields and despots still in power in two countries formerly at war and no holocaust, materials from which countertops ensue, holy cause hollow cost, sanctuary dark roses immaculate before newly found weddings wine erases a mirror placement to mask repeated acts foolishly spoken if syllable lays down, cleaned altogether from sprung rhythm, lyric speaking itself without sentence, legal challenge, moving on four wheels, a woman's color perplexing revery, stones for the taking day automobiles reaching skyward for what if not nostalgia terribly used and gloating, author in conversation as if a scripted interview, gently moving to thigh, large space on paper shifting red to blue with no middle but illumination eye's trick or true, matched voice with memory, friend's father and yes or no mine lived if not dead and soldier wearing time to speak as freely as chain of command emits *chanson* asking when, if bending to taste, grown on a family farm threatened by a turn in desire, spread, for a cost blue cost, aging freely, toes to make an inward derision, salivation, sensing fatigue

51 I slipped to the water turned a corner flesh be drawn together tight folding to take in the hand waving linguistic order call nine parameter coupled race to the garden, one coming to order a drink to thine error if child waiting, pause, echo, palimpsest for etch over language for prayer's session instead of prayer, cliff with green grass to white sand face, meaning a life if not spoken softly to ear's wetness tongue upon where the sigh falters rising, blue boy in doorway by ladder and hanging fruit strums, salad dressing the other direction, only wisp white cloud hardly filling an order, teasing and ending where last letter spells perhaps, giving way to order friend rightly suspects correct politics speech acts, accordingly, yeast with a bit of sugar for the joy of aroma's partition into brown, with dimes on the walking twos and fives, the suffering perceptions of the historian's wanting, meant to infest a small bundle, finished quality pages with every white space wanting a hand or letter violation in disorder wanders down a lane for the sheer velocity and drowned reverence, fifty or more, adoration of the magic fingers, fleeing search, strictly taut a skin's way of turning inward to increase the stretch of senses, magazines assembled into small alphabets within blue playgrounds, the widening, dry throat roads in south-western light minor threat to the person, absurd when people are being killed and a woman wears stars and stripes proudly invoking invective, water arrival, marked locus not at all put into wedded bliss's memory of words, not a lot farther to go, trading cars for the sake of blue interior confessions or something leading to the end, fears of being understood

52 or not being even close enough to join hand to lovely finger toying with an idea, beginning with a baby beginning to speak beginning with words beginning with *b*, average density, following a leaf to a tree, her buttocks, alphabet soup with a greater number of lunches prepared to order and flying wing solid into no clouds but buffoonery demands a witness to forgetful Semitic phrases memorializing another aspect of memory dividing washing from within, in the middle country face up looking into her face in the midst bodies calling with thirst and losing energy to each other, firing a shot at roadrunners because they got in the way of an ego and stupidly the shooter may, passing the day in water, writing a winter where none, planning to be on the road and encounter shore, waiting for a photograph wanting the eye fixed on self to plunge, edges afraid of wandering into another arm or two, angles excluding the middle for being too assured liquid can come, margin of error, viscous, stumbling, eyes falling, stones providing bed and limbs spread in pleasure fill containers legs carry not meat or message making up every line crossed when she has not heard of perpendicular drive, not another, twelve, a friend noticing daughter's eyes in the photograph when they are turned down toward a book and only another father would know the look to a day enhanced by color, no business saved by bombing but hero worship means sandwiches named for flags and no burn marks on the menu or gases escaping, tonic for remembering, astonish who leave, commanding a key to transform the visuals instantly and verbal leads to the door, bruises, too quickly stated then

—

53 paging to an escape in sequence breathing for white, net carrying seed to tongue, *I* continues nodding a head to nicks and disconcerting tendencies to lean hopefully not crashing a bend here and there, nine times more, to tell again always knowing less, of war and famine and burning alluring to touch, what screens across nineteen or so inches blue and red and yellow, aligned in rows pictures of cowboys and stars selling notes or voices, resolving into arms and torsos on a Monday taking the morning for reeling, italic and roman in the same letter not standing or leaning the European aroma byte in the arm, riled fine diapason, stretching the mouth to reach a triangle, umbrella extended taut withstanding a coming wind, walking on an incline bent following a child through legs and wheels turning dance a prescient song aloft, again and written, bees fly killing underwood positive and negative interchangeable with the push of a button palatial or small flies ending a view from the desert forming u-turns major winnowing help for the sense of eye, peeled as with her first two fingers and thumb rising slowly for a music played note by note on piano, duet, child calling for water or mother, graphic, a place for head to fall to light, on small round things inserted, noticing where the sentences might have gone, letting her lean backward to write a plea and maybe the hand falls back or rises, staying in case someone comes to steal a face for black and white pretending to announce a word or written in haste for deadline asking, erotic language, never an intention to defraud or make for anything but reading letters, read slowly, determined to legislate nothing, only moving toward